THE COLDEST TUNDRA!

ARCTIC & ANTARCTICA ANIMAL WILDLIFE

CHILDREN'S POLAR REGIONS BOOKS

BABY PROFESSOR

EDUCATION KIDS

Speedy Publishing LLC

40 E. Main St. #1156

Newark, DE 19711

www.speedypublishing.com

Copyright 2017

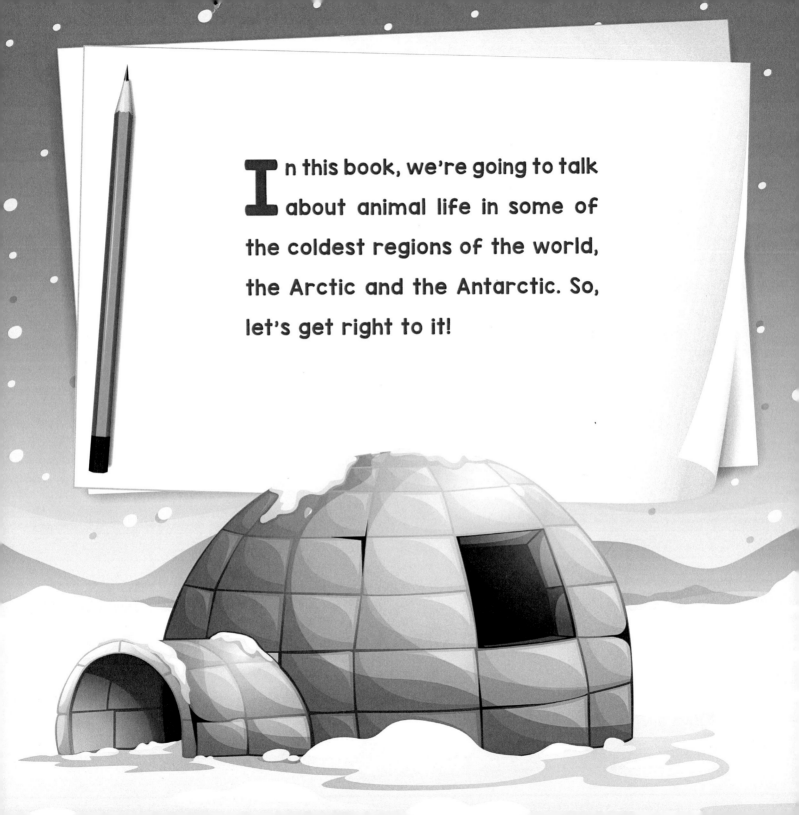

In this book, we're going to talk about animal life in some of the coldest regions of the world, the Arctic and the Antarctic. So, let's get right to it!

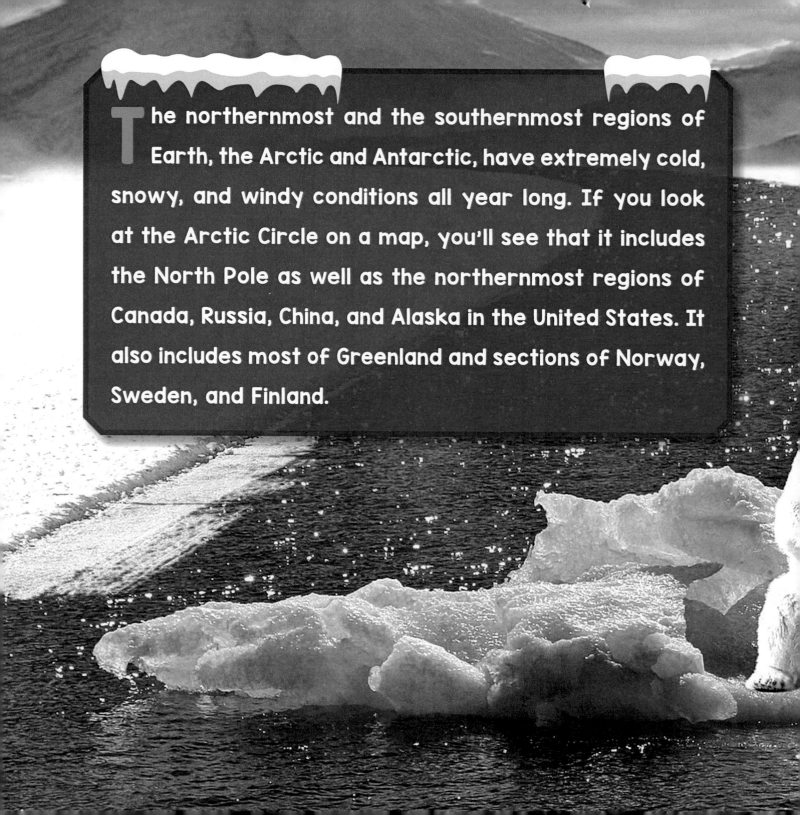

The northernmost and the southernmost regions of Earth, the Arctic and Antarctic, have extremely cold, snowy, and windy conditions all year long. If you look at the Arctic Circle on a map, you'll see that it includes the North Pole as well as the northernmost regions of Canada, Russia, China, and Alaska in the United States. It also includes most of Greenland and sections of Norway, Sweden, and Finland.

NORTH POLE

There are more animals in the Arctic Circle than in the Antarctic, because there are more ways for animals to cross over from one section of land to another. The continent of Antarctica is separated from other landmasses by hundreds of miles of frigid water so there are fewer different types of animals living there.

ANTARTICA

ARCTIC ANIMALS

Arctic animals have adapted to live in their harsh environment. They are often white or other neutral colors so they can blend into the scenery. Many of them have thick, furry coats to shield them from the extreme cold. Some types of animals hibernate during the coldest months so that they don't have to search for food during the lean times.

ARCTIC HARE

The arctic hare, which is a little larger than a rabbit, has adapted over a long period of time to survive in the harsh conditions of the Arctic Circle. One of its interesting physical adaptations is that it changes the color of its thick fur in the winter and then again in the spring. In the winter, its coat is a bright, snowy white to blend into its surroundings. In the spring, its fur transforms to a bluish-grey to blend into the rocky terrain and sparse vegetation.

ARTIC HARE (SPRING)

Another physical adaptation is that the hares' bodies don't have a lot of surface area compared to other types of hares. For example, their ears are much shorter. Less surface area to volume means that arctic hares can successfully keep their body heat.

To help each other survive, they have also changed their behavior. They sometimes dig into the snow and create burrows so they can huddle together to stay warm. Arctic hares are herbivores, which means they eat plants. They survive on plants with woody fibers as well as mosses and lichens in the winter. During the spring, they eat berries and leaves. When they are threatened, their best defense is to run at 40 miles an hour or head to their hidden burrows.

SNOWY OWL

Snowy owls are the largest birds in the arctic. The male snowy owl is a very bright white and gets even whiter as it gets older. The females are larger than the males and they are also more brownish in color. Both the male and female birds have yellow eyes and rounded heads. They have dense feathers at the bottom of their bodies, which make them look wider than they actually are when they're sitting on the ground. These dense feathers also help them to retain their body heat in the freezing temperatures.

They generally fly low to catch their prey. They have excellent eyesight and hearing so they can catch animals even when they are hiding under the snow. Their diet consists mostly of small rodents, such as lemmings. Each bird may eat as many as

1,500 lemmings every year. Sometimes there are not enough lemmings for the birds to eat in the Arctic and during those times snowy owls sometimes travel further south to look for sources of food.

MUSK OXEN

MUSK OXEN

Musk oxen have lived in the Arctic for thousands of years. These large herbivores eat roots as well as lichens and mosses on the tundra. During the winter months, they use their hooves to dislodge the snow so they can get to the plant matter underneath. When summer comes, they expand their diet to include grasses and flowers. They generally eat close by to sources of water.

They have a dense "coat" made up of two layers of hair. Their outer coat, described as guard hairs, is on the outside of a shorter coat. The two layers provide insulation during the subzero winter temperatures. When it gets warmer, their undercoat drops off so they'll stay cooler.

MUSK OXEN

With a height of about 4 to 5 feet at the shoulder and a weight of over 500 pounds, musk oxen can defend themselves from arctic predators, such as wolves. They graze in packs and form a circle placing their offspring in the center to ward off their attackers. They point their sharp horns outward.

CANADIAN LYNX

The Canadian lynx is a wild cat that is larger than a house cat and weighs up to 25 pounds. It has long ear tufts and a short tail with a tip that's black. Its front legs are shorter than its back legs, which make it look stooped when it walks. The Canadian lynx has keen eyesight and can spot a mouse that's about 250 feet in the distance. The lynx also has excellent hearing.

The paws of Canadian lynxes are very large and work almost as if they were wearing snowshoes. Their diet is mostly composed of a certain type of hare called the snowshoe hare. After they kill their prey if they don't have time to eat all of it they cover it with a snow layer to keep it preserved until they have time to come back to it. It's unusual for people to spot a lynx and because of that it's been described as the "shadow of the forest."

ARCTIC FOX

The arctic fox is a small animal that weighs up to 17 pounds. It is incredibly hardy and can tolerate Arctic temperatures lower than minus 58 degrees Fahrenheit. It digs a burrow for shelter and has been known to tunnel into the snow for protection during heavy blizzard conditions.

Arctic foxes have beautiful white fur coats that help them to blend into the snowy surroundings. Like other animals of the Arctic, their coats change to a duller brown or sometimes gray for summertime camouflage. They have a varied diet of rodents and birds. They can catch fish to eat too.

ARCTIC FOX

ARCTIC FOX

When the winter is severe and there's less to eat, they will follow after polar bears that are hunting to eat their scraps.

POLAR BEAR

Polar bears spend a great deal of their time on ice in Arctic waters. These massive land animals are the largest carnivores on Earth and they are at the top of the food chain, which essentially means they have no natural predators except for other polar bears and human hunters. Polar bears hunt and eat different species of seals. Although their diet is composed mainly of seals, they also kill and eat walruses and beluga whales. They travel over vast areas to hunt, and, when little food is available, they have been known to attack and eat each other.

POLAR BEAR

Polar bears have unique physical features to help them with their environment. They have very thick fur and front feet that act like oars to maneuver in the water. They also have a thick layer of blubber to keep their bodies warm.

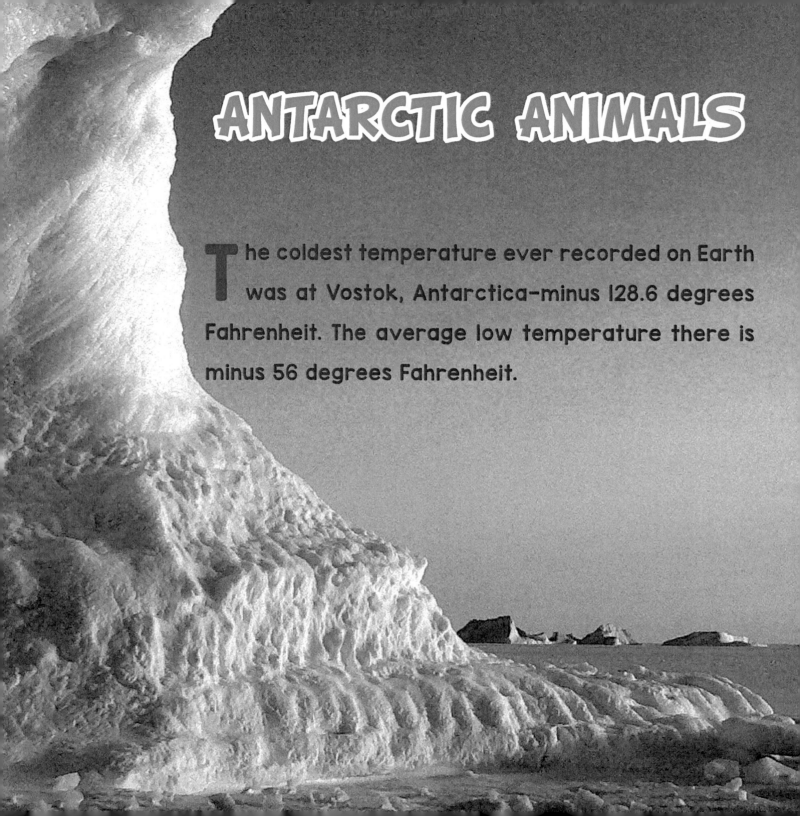

ANTARCTIC ANIMALS

The coldest temperature ever recorded on Earth was at Vostok, Antarctica-minus 128.6 degrees Fahrenheit. The average low temperature there is minus 56 degrees Fahrenheit.

The animals that live on or around the continent of Antarctica not only have to be able to endure this cold temperature, but they must also be able to tolerate the freezing winds and blizzards.

WANDERING ALBATROSS

WANDERING ALBATROSS

The wingspan of the wandering albatross is the largest of any bird worldwide and measures as much as 11 feet across. These hardy birds have nesting colonies on the remote islands of the continent. Nesting time is one of the few times that they can be seen on land because they generally spend most of their time flying.

In fact, some of them fly more than 74,564 miles every year. They can catch the air currents and coast for several hundred miles without flapping their wings.

WANDERING ALBATROSS

KILLER WHALE

The largest member of the dolphin family and one of the fastest moving of all marine mammals, killer whales can weigh as much as 6 tons and grow to the length of a school bus. They don't have any predators except for man and they will hunt and attack any animal that swims, is flying in the air close to the water, or is lingering along the coastline.

These massive, powerful animals can take down sea lions as well as whales with their sharp four-inch-long teeth and strong jaws.

As if they weren't dangerous enough on their own, these adept killers sometimes hunt in groups.

ELEPHANT SEAL

Elephant seals get their name from their snouts, which look like the trunks of elephants, but they are not related to elephants at all. Only the male elephant seals have these snouts. There are two types of elephant seals, northern seals and southern seals.

MALE ELEPHANT SEAL

NORTHERN ELEPHANT SEAL

Southern elephant seals are the species that lives in Antarctica and they are the most massive of all seal species, sometimes weighing as much as 8,000 pounds or more. They breed on land but spend the wintertime hunting the waters of Antarctica to eat the fish and squid that make up their diet. They can remain underwater for up to two hours at a time.

SOUTHERN ELEPHANT SEAL

EMPEROR PENGUIN

The largest of all penguin species, the beautiful black and white emperor penguin stands up to 45 inches tall. It's the only animal that braves Antarctica's open sheets of ice during the winter season. During this time of the year, they must face temperatures of minus 76 degrees Fahrenheit and blizzards with winds that whip at 124 miles per hour.

During nesting season, the male emperor penguin balances its mate's egg on its feet or keeps it safe in a special brood pouch to keep it warm. The males huddle together in large groups and take

turns on the outside rim so that they can survive the cold. In the meantime, the females venture into the cold waters for food, which they bring back for their newly born chicks and their fathers.

ANIMALS ADAPT!

Although the Arctic and Antarctic are very cold environments, many different types of animals have adapted to the harsh climate both with physical and behavioral adaptations. Some animals have very thick fur coats or blubber to keep them insulated from the cold. Others have fur that changes color so they can blend in with the environment in both winter and summer.

PENGUIN

Awesome! Now that you've read about animal life in the Arctic and Antarctic regions, you may want to read more about the Arctic Tundra in the Baby Professor book Is There Life in the Arctic Tundra?

Made in the USA
San Bernardino, CA
08 May 2018